CONTENTS

Introduction	4
The natural landscape	6
Climate and natural vegetation	8
Towns and cities	10
City life in Spain	12
Farming landscapes	14
Family farming	16
What's in Spanish shops?	18
Spanish cooking	20
Made in Spain	22
Transport and travel	24
Leisure and sport	26
Customs and arts	28
Spain Factfile	30
Glossary	31
Index	32

INTRODUCTION

The Iberian peninsula

Spain covers an area of 504,782 square kilometres. It takes up over 80% of the area of the Iberian **peninsula**. The Iberian peninsula is surrounded by the Mediterranean Sea, the Atlantic Ocean and the Bay of Biscay. Spain shares the peninsula with Portugal, its neighbour to the west. It is joined to France and the rest of Europe by a stretch of land that is about 400 kilometres wide.

Spain is the second biggest country in Western Europe, but it is one of the least crowded. On average, there are only 78 people per square kilometre compared to 105 in France and 239 in the United Kingdom. This figure is called the population density.

Spanish history

Spain was part of the Roman Empire for almost 600 years. Then in AD711, it was invaded and conquered by Muslim Arabs called Moors. The country divided into different kingdoms whose inhabitants often fought against each other.

The city of Seville in Andalucía [anda-luTHIA].
- *The tower is the Torre de Oro which was built by the Moors.*
- *It is said to have been covered by gold when it was built.*

The Christian cathedral at Santiago de Compostela.
- *There is a week-long festival at Santiago every year in July.*

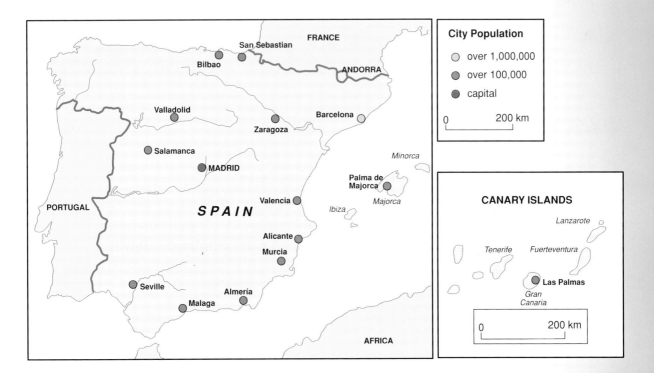

In 1492, Spain became one united country. This was the same year that Christopher Columbus sailed from Spain to cross the Atlantic Ocean. Spanish conquests in North and South America, as well as South-East Asia, gave it great wealth and a worldwide empire. In the 19th century Spain lost land to France and England in expensive wars. Then more land was lost when its American **colonies** rebelled and became independent.

Modern Spain

In 1930, the king was expelled and Spain was declared a **republic**. But then the Spanish people suffered terrible fighting during the **civil war** of 1936-1939. The **fascists** won and Spain had a new leader, the **dictator** General Franco. When Franco died in 1975, Spain became a **monarchy** again when Juan Carlos agreed to be king. Since then, Spain has joined the Economic Union (EU) with other European countries. Working with these countries is helping to make Spain wealthy again. Two events in 1992: Expo'92 in Seville and the Summer Oympics in Barcelona [bartha-LOna], have also helped to create more jobs and make Spain even more popular with tourists.

Some regions in Spain have their own languages and regional governments. The Basque region in the western Pyrenees and north-east coast of Spain is one of these regions. Some people who live there want to form a separate country. Catalonia is another of these regions, with Barcelona as its regional capital city.

THE NATURAL LANDSCAPE

Spain's uplands

An upland area called the Meseta covers most of Spain. The Meseta is a huge **plateau** about 600 metres above sea level. The edges of the Meseta drop down to narrow coastal lowlands.

Several parts of Spain rise high above the Meseta. In the north, there are the Cantabrian Mountains. In the north-east, the Pyrenees Mountains form a barrier between Spain and France across the neck of the **peninsula**. The Pyrenees Mountains rise to just over 3000 metres with the highest peak at 3404 metres. Mountain ranges called **sierras** stretch across the Meseta dividing it into two. In the south, the snowy Sierra Nevada has the highest point on mainland Spain at 3478 metres high.

The island landscapes

The Balearic Islands of Majorca [my-orka], Ibiza [i-beetha], Minorca, Cabrera and Formentera are owned by Spain. These lie about 200 kilometres off the south coast of Spain.

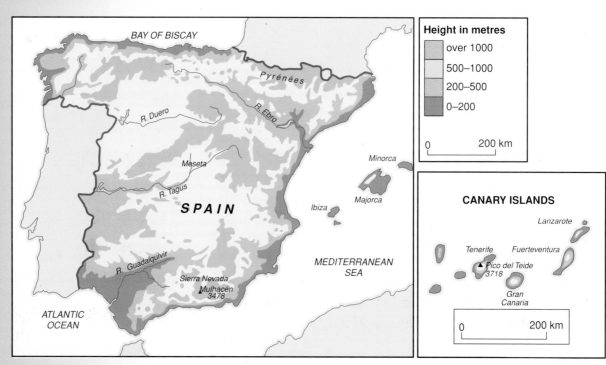

Height in metres

	over 1000
	500–1000
	200–500
	0–200

0   200 km

BAY OF BISCAY

Pyrénées

R. Duero

R. Ebro

Meseta

R. Tagus

SPAIN

R. Guadalquivir

Sierra Nevada
Mulhacén
3478

ATLANTIC
OCEAN

Minorca

Majorca

Ibiza

MEDITERRANEAN
SEA

CANARY ISLANDS

Lanzarote

Tenerife   Fuerteventura

Pico del Teide
3718

Gran
Canaria

0   200 km

Pico del Teide on Tenerife in the Canary Islands.
- *The mountains are volcanoes that pour out dark coloured lava.*

The landscape of La Mancha on the Meseta.
- *Windmills were used to grind grains of wheat into flour as well as pump water up from underground.*

The highest point of land owned by Spain is the Pico del Teide in the Canary Islands, which rises to 3718 metres. Pico del Teide is on the popular holiday island of Tenerife. The Canary Islands are in the Atlantic Ocean about 100 kilometres off the coast of north-west Africa. Most of the seven Canary Islands are the remains of old volcanoes. Many of their beaches are made from black sand. This comes from dark volcanic **lava** that has been worn away by the waves and weather.

River landscapes

The rivers Duero, Tagus and Guadiana cut valleys through the Meseta plateau, flow through Portugal then out into the Atlantic. The largest river on the peninsula is the Tagus. It flows for 1100 kilometres through Spain before passing through Portugal to enter the sea.

Some of the major river valleys, such as the Ebro and Guadalquivir, have rich soils which are good for farming. However, many of the smaller rivers dry up during the summer when there is just not enough rain to keep them flowing. Some rivers have cut such steep ravines into the landscape that the valley bottoms are difficult to farm and **irrigate**.

The Canary Islands take their name from the Latin word *canes* which means dogs. Wild dogs used to live on the islands. Canary birds were named after the Canary Islands, one of their homes in the wild.

CLIMATE AND NATURAL VEGETATION

A hotel on the Costa del Sol on the most southerly part of mainland Spain.
* *Hot summer weather makes this area ideal for tourists.*

Types of climate

Spain is known for having hot, cloudless and dry summers. On the Meseta, summer is very hot and dry. But in winter, temperatures can reach freezing point. There are two main reasons for this. One is that the Meseta is higher than the coastal lowlands. The second is that places away from the sea cool down much more quickly than coastal areas.

Along the Mediterranean coast and the Balearic Islands, the temperature on a summer's day is likely to be about 30°C. Even in winter, the temperature can be mild at about 10°C, although it is often wet. These figures are typical for a Mediterranean climate.

In the north of Spain, it is usually wetter and a little cooler in both summer and winter. This is called a **temperate** climate. The mountain areas are also wetter and cooler.

Forest and scrub

Most of Spain's forests are in the mountain ranges in the north where it is cooler and wetter. Oak and other **deciduous** trees grow there. In the south, pine trees survive the dry climate by having tough, needle-like leaves that reduce water loss. Much of the rest of Spain is scrubland called *matorral* or *garrigue* where there are scattered low bushes and short grasses.

Wildlife

In Spain, there are a few areas where wild animals can live, especially the larger ones such as the ibex, a goat-like animal that lives in mountain areas. There are also small numbers of brown bears, wolves, wild cats and wild boars, animals that have died out in northern Europe. In Spain, these animals are now protected by **conservation** laws and there are five **national parks** to protect the country's wildlife. Some rare species still live in the wild, such as flamingos and the magnificent Spanish imperial eagle, and animals such as tarantula spiders, red deer, boar and a rare lynx. They are conserved in the Coto Doñana National Park in the south.

A rubbish dump near Madrid has become a feeding ground for up to 100,000 birds including ravens, kites and storks. Some storks stay on the dump over the winter. They use strips of bin-liners for their nests.

The landscape of Andalucía near Alicante.
- *There is scrub vegetation on the dry and rocky soils.*
- *Farmers grow citrus trees such as lemons and oranges.*

TOWNS AND CITIES

The old town of Marcilla,
[mar-THEE-lya] in Navarra.
• *The combination of ancient*
  medieval walls and modern
  paving is a common sight.

Town history

Within most towns and cities in Spain there are styles of buildings which remain from different periods in its history. The Romans built walled towns which were easy to defend. The Moors built finely decorated palaces and mosques such as the Great Mosque in Cordoba and the Alhambra Palace in Granada.

In medieval times, castles and city walls were built. There are cathedrals from the 16th and 17th centuries, as well as long avenues and squares called *plazas.* Most Spanish towns and cities today have large Roman Catholic cathedrals and churches. The *plazas* are now surrounded by shops and streets which come to life in the evenings as families and friends come out to meet.

Madrid and Barcelona

All distances in Spain are measured from a stone in the centre of Madrid called *kilómetro cero.* In 1561, King Philip II of Spain made Madrid the country's **capital city**. He thought that the best place for a capital city was in the centre of the country. Madrid is now a city with just over three million people and it is still the country's capital.

The city and tourist resort of Alicante in the south of Spain.
- *Many of the buildings are newly built for the tourist industry.*
- *The Santa Barbara castle overlooks the city from a rocky hill. It was built by the Moors.*

About 60 million tourists visit Spain every year. This is more than the total of 37 million people who live in Spain. Eight out of every ten visitors only go to the coastal areas along the Mediterranean Sea. This includes the Balearic and the Canary Islands.

Barcelona is one of the main industrial cities and Spain's biggest port. It is also the capital of Catalonia. Its oldest buildings and medieval walls are around the harbour itself. The city has grown far beyond the old walls and now has a population of just under two million people.

Tourist resorts

There used to be a large number of small fishing ports along the Mediterranean coast. Many of them are now busy and noisy **holiday resorts** with high-rise hotels, holiday flats, restaurants and night-clubs. Benidorm on the Costa Blanca and Malaga on the Costa del Sol are two such resorts. Airports at places like Malaga, Alicante and Gerona have made the resorts easy to get to for people looking for beaches and summer sunshine.

CITY LIFE IN SPAIN

Valencia, the business city

Valencia is the main city on the Costa Del Azahar on the east coast of Spain. It is a popular holiday area, with sandy beaches and orange groves. It is also a city where many people work in offices or the car-making and printing industries.

The Grijalvo [gree-HALbo] family live in a suburb of Valencia. It takes about half an hour to drive to the city centre from their home. They live high up in a block of flats where they have lived for two years.
The neighbourhood is a pleasant area with a pedestrian precinct, trees and recreation areas. There are good shops for food and most of the other family needs.

The Grijalvo family on the balcony of their apartment in Valencia.

Cati and her husband Manuel both have good jobs in Valencia. Cati works in the University of Valencia where she is in charge of administration. She drives to work in one of the family's two cars.
Manuel works as a sales manager for a publishing company in the city centre. This is a UK company that has branches in many different countries. They employ a cleaner to help with the housework.

Manu plays football for the Serranos Football Club.

Begoña at her ballet class.
- *Ballet dancing is a good way to keep fit and meet friends.*

The family's day

The Grijalvo family get up at about 6.30 am then have breakfast. This is usually just a cup of coffee or hot chocolate and some biscuits. They all go to work or school, and apart from Manuel, they come home again at about 5.30 pm. The evening meal is at about 7.00 pm. Manuel sometimes works for over 10 hours a day, so they often do not see him until late.

The local shop
- *There is a good range of food and other shops in the neighbourhood.*

Manu and Begoña

The two children are Manu, who is aged 12, and Begoña, aged 10. They both go to the same school in Valencia. This is a school that takes children from nursery age up to 16 years.

Manu's favourite sport is football. He plays for the local junior team, called the Serranos Football Club. When he is older, he will be able to play for the club's older teams.

Begoña enjoys ballet dancing. She goes to ballet lessons at the Centro de Danza (dance centre) in Valencia. Perhaps one day Begoña will become a famous ballerina and Manu will be a football star. It is more likely that they will both find good jobs in the many offices and factories in one of Spain's most dynamic cities.

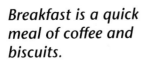

Breakfast is a quick meal of coffee and biscuits.

FARMING LANDSCAPES

The farming landscape in north-east Spain.
- *Farmers are growing wheat in large fields.*
- *The dry summer climate helps the wheat ripen.*

Farmers in Spain

About 50 years ago, just over half the people working in Spain worked on farms. Farms were either very small and owned by **peasants**, or were very big and owned by rich landowners. Now only one person in every ten works in farming. The size of farms has also changed. The smaller farms are being bought up and combined while many of the very largest farms have been broken up and made smaller.

Traditional crops

Spain is among the world's top ten countries for growing a wide range of produce. It has a long history of growing grapes for wine. Spain is still the world's third largest maker of wine. Sherry is a special type of wine named after a town called Jerez [he-reth] de la Frontera in Spain. Cork comes from cork oak trees to be used in wine and sherry bottles.

The climate in Spain is also suited to growing fruit, especially **citrus fruits** such as oranges and lemons. Spain is the world's fourth largest orange producer and the fifth largest lemon and lime producer. It is the world's second largest producer of olive oil.

There are 167 million olive trees in Spain. This is one fifth of all the olive trees in the world.

The Meseta **plateau** is an open landscape where grain crops such as wheat, barley and sunflowers are grown. Sheep graze on land that is too poor to rear cattle. Small windmills are a common sight. They are used to pump water from below the ground or for grinding grain, though many are now disused.

Irrigation and vegetables

The long dry summers are always a problem for Spanish farmers. In some years, there is even a **drought** in winter. This is why there is more **irrigated** land in Spain than anywhere else in Europe. The Moors brought methods of irrigation to Spain over 1000 years ago. The water comes from rivers, reservoirs or from underground.

In some areas, small irrigated farms called *huertas* are used to grow more than one crop of vegetables each year. Crops such as water melons, tomatoes, strawberries and cucumbers are grown using irrigation water. They are driven by refrigerated lorry to countries in northern Europe. This is why supermarkets in the United Kingdom are able to sell fresh fruit and vegetables, even in winter.

A farmer is checking his vines.
- *Other crops on his farm include sweetcorn and cabbages.*

FAMILY FARMING

The Merino family and some friends at home.
- *People in country areas work together and get to know each other very well.*

The family farm

Manolo and Javier [ha-BYER] Merino, their uncle Enrique and mother Chelo own a special type of farm. They breed bulls, not for meat, but to be used in sport. There are about 300 bulls on the farm. A few years ago, Chelo's husband was killed by one of the bulls. Now the remaining members of the family, with some helpers, are running the farm. The Merino family has been on this farm for the last 60 years.

The farm is in the countryside near a small town called Marcilla. This is near Pamplona, in the north of Spain. Pamplona is famous for its festival when bulls are made to run through the streets for sport. The family also breed bulls for bullfighting. These fighting bulls are called *Toros de lidia*.

Bulls need to be reared so they grow to be strong and able to fight. This means they have to be fed properly. There is often little rainfall in this area so good grass does not grow well. Instead, they are fed a mixture of grass and bean stalks, that are waste material from a nearby frozen-food factory. The bulls are fed this mixture three times every day. It is no wonder that they grow to become so powerful.

Bulls on the Merino's farm are fed on bean stalks from a local factory.
- *Bulls have to weigh about 460 kg before they can enter the bull ring.*

The local vet
- *The bulls have to be looked after by a vet to make sure they are fit for the bull ring.*
- *Sharp horns make them dangerous to work with.*

The family home

The family do not live on their farm. They live in a small flat on a narrow street in Marcilla. Chelo does most of her shopping in small shops in the town.

The family have breakfast at about 7.00 am then travel out to the farm to work. At about 2.00 pm, they go back to the village for a meal and then go back to the farm until about 8.30 pm. Their main meal of the day is in the evening around 9.00 o'clock.

A village shop in the town of Marcilla.
- *The SPAR name is familiar to people in many other countries in Europe.*

Village life-style

Running the farm is a difficult job that does not leave much time for recreation. Manolo and Javier sometimes go horse riding and after their evening meal, they like to go to a local bar to meet their friends.

The two Merino brothers are now 17 and 19. They both went to a primary school but did not go on to secondary school. They went to work on the farm with their father. In the past, this often happened in country areas. Keeping up the family farm was more important than getting qualifications in school. Nobody in the family travels much outside Marcilla. Everything this family want is either on their farm or in their town.

WHAT'S IN SPANISH SHOPS?

Spending more

About 30 years ago, Spain was one of the poorest countries in Western Europe. Most Spanish people did not have enough money to spend on anything except their basic needs. For these people, most of their shopping was done in the local village shops and markets. Now money earned from tourism and new industry has helped give people more money and a better **standard of living**.

A supermarket in Barcelona.
- *There are jars of olives, tins of fish and packets of different types of convenience foods.*

The most expensive shops in Spain today are the big city department stores and specialist shops. The *El Corte Inglés* stores found in the major cities are the best known department stores. These shops sell most things, including high quality clothes, some made out of fur and leather.

Market shopping

Supermarkets are becoming increasingly popular, although many Spanish shoppers still prefer to buy fresh food from a street market or purpose-built covered market. Freshly caught fish and fresh vegetables and fruit are sold from colourful market stalls. Clothes and shoes can also be bought in the markets.

The Rastro market in Madrid is a very popular place to go on Sundays. You can buy just about anything at this lively market selling second-hand goods.

*Street bars and
stalls in Valencia.*
- *Shoppers are able
to buy fresh food
grown on nearby farms.*

Small local shops

There are still many small, local
shops in both the cities and in country
towns and villages. Local bakers bake the
fresh bread which is eaten with most meals.
The smell of freshly made cakes comes from
the local *pastelería*. There are also small
shops selling different types of meat,
sausages and vegetables.

Many local grocery shops are now run like
small supermarkets – they sell a wider range
of goods than they used to.

Shops usually open at about 9.30 am then
close at 2 pm. This is when many people go
home for a meal and for a short sleep called
a *siesta* during the heat of the early
afternoon. The shops open again at
about 4.30 pm and stay open until 8 pm.

The *siesta* is a custom that is slowly
changing as people work in air-conditioned
offices and factories and do business with
people in other countries who are still at
work at lunchtime.

**One way to measure the
wealth of a country is by its
Gross National Product. This
measures the value of all
the goods produced there in
a year. These figures are
usually given in one form of
money, American dollars, so
that it is easy to make
comparisons between
countries. For example, each
person in Spain produces
about $13,590 of goods.**

SPANISH COOKING

Food traditions

Traditions in cooking food are passed on through families over hundreds of years. In the past, the type of food eaten in an area depended on what was grown locally. This is what gives each region its own unique dishes. Many of these traditional foods are still made, though food and drinks are becoming more international. Coca Cola is as popular in Spain as it is in other countries.

Paella is [pa-ELya] one of Spain's best known dishes. It comes from Valencia on the Mediterranean coast. In Latin, the word paella means a pan. Fish such as anchovies and prawns or sometimes pieces of meat, are fried in a pan with peppers, vegetables and rice.

The rice turns yellow when the yellow-coloured flavouring called saffron is added to it. Other dishes using cod and eels are popular. They are caught near the fishing ports in the Bay of Biscay.

Tapas meals

There are small bars called tapas bars all over Spain. A *tapa* is a small plate of food eaten as a snack. It is usually served with a drink, especially in southern Spain. Each bar has its own way of making the tapas. Some serve fried mushrooms with prawns and peppers. Others have slices of cold meat, nuts and vegetables.

Eating out in Valencia.
- *Eating paella directly from the pan with a wooden spoon.*

Tourists enjoying a cool beer in the shade.
• *Some people prefer to retire to the cool of a bar for their siesta.*

Mahón is the main town on the Balearic island of Menorca. This is where the word mayonnaise comes from. It was a sauce originally made in Mahón.

Omelettes

Tortillas (omelettes) are a favourite Spanish dish. They are usually made from beaten eggs that are cooked in olive oil in a frying pan. Slices of onions, potatoes or different types of vegetables are often added to *tortillas. Tortillas* can be eaten either straight from the pan, or cold as a snack or part of a picnic.

Staying cool

The hot climate in Spain helps explain why the cold but spicy soup called *gazpacho* is popular. *Gazpacho* is made from tomatoes, onions, garlic, hot spices and other chopped vegetables. Other drinks to beat the heat include *cerveza* [ther-BE-tha], (beer) and fizzy drinks. In the south, sherry is served chilled, often with a *tapa* of olives. All over Spain, coffee is taken black and very strong in small cups. A popular party or evening drink is *sangría,* in which wine is mixed with juices and chunks of fruit.

MADE IN SPAIN

Crafts and wine

There is a long history of **craft industries** in Spain. As in other European countries today, these industries, such as lace-making for traditional costumes and guitar-making for flamenco and classical music, are declining. Such products are now mostly made for the tourist market. Modern machinery has replaced the skilled workers.

Wine-making is an example of a traditional **food processing** industry. Sherry is a special type of wine. The sherry is put in casks and left to **ferment** in a warehouse.

This *bodega* is usually found underground where it is cooler. Modern methods of making wine and sherry use machinery and metal casks. However, much of the wine is still fermented in casks made from oak. This helps give the wine a special flavour.

Industrial Spain

Modern industry in Spain is mainly in the largest towns and cities such as Madrid, Barcelona and Bilbao. Cloth and clothes are **mass produced** instead of being made by hand.

A bottling plant for Rioja wine.
- *Making and exporting wine is one of Spain's main food processing industries.*

Iron and steel is produced and used in the car and ship-building industries. The low wages paid to Spanish workers (compared to workers in other European countries), has helped keep down the price of goods made in Spain.

Almost two million cars are made in Spain each year. This is about one car every four minutes during a year. SEAT cars are made in Spain and exported to other European countries. Foreign companies, such as Ford and General Motors, have opened car assembly factories in Spain. In some factories, parts are made for cars that are assembled in other countries such as in the United Kingdom. This is done so that each piece can be mass produced to keep down the costs.

An EU member

Spain became a member of the European Union (EU) in 1986. Members of the EU buy goods from each other without paying **import taxes**. It is a challenge for Spanish industry to keep up with the standards of other EU countries. Soon there may be only half the present number of shipyard workers. What will happen to all those who are made unemployed?

Look through some books you use in school and find out where they are printed. You will probably find some that are printed and bound in Spain. Printing is one of Spain's biggest industries.

Hundreds of the new Ka model lined up outside the Ford factory in Valencia.

TRANSPORT AND TRAVEL

Road communications

A modern industrial country must have good **communications** between different places. This is why so much is being done to improve all kinds of transport in Spain. There are still some unpaved country roads and some farmers still use donkeys and carts. However, such sights are becoming more and more unusual.

Main roads and motorways radiate out from Madrid to all the other main cities. There is a **toll** to pay on some of the motorways. A drive from Madrid to Barcelona takes about eight hours. It takes about six hours to drive to Seville.

Cars and lorries provide the main transport for people and goods. New roads have been particularly important along the south coast. This is because of the millions of tourists who go there every year. These new roads by-pass the town centres of holiday resorts, such as Torremolinos and Marbella.

The railway terminal in Seville.
Most of Spain's trains run on wide-gauge railway tracks.
- *The wide gauge was chosen to stop any invading army using trains to enter Spain.*

Almost 60% of tourists to Spain travel by road across the Pyrenees Mountains from France. About one in every three tourists comes by plane as part of a package holiday to either the Mediterranean coast or to the islands.

Trams have their own 'roads' and platforms on the streets of Valencia.
- *Electric trams are quiet and do not pollute the atmosphere.*

Rail links

There is also a rail network that radiates out from Madrid. A special fast route has been built between the main cities such as Madrid and Seville. This journey now takes 2 hours and 55 minutes, at speeds of up to 250 kilometres per hour.

The fastest and most luxurious trains are TALGO trains. Local routes use slower *expresos* trains with *electrotrén* trains on longer distance routes.

Travel to Spain

Tourism is one of the main ways that Spain earns money. There are airports near all the main holiday areas, including airports near Palma on Majorca and Tenerife in the Canary Islands. **Ferry boats** sail between Plymouth in the United Kingdom and Santander in northern Spain.

LEISURE AND SPORT

The sporting scene

More people than ever before in Spain are watching or taking part in sport, and especially football. The football matches at clubs such as Real Madrid and Barcelona attract huge crowds. These clubs have won many cups in Spain and also in international competitions.

Also, success by top international players, such as Arantxa [aRAN-cha] Sanchez in tennis and Severiano Ballesteros in golf, have helped to make these popular sports. Now, many visitors to Spain come especially for golfing and tennis coaching courses.

Ancient sports

Pelota is an ancient game played in Spain. The game is played like squash in a court called a *frontón.* A wicker basket called a *cesta,* or a bat called a *pala* is used to fire a ball against the *frontón* wall. Sometimes *pelota* is played like handball without a bat or basket. The game is especially popular in the north-east Basque region of Spain.

A bullfight in Alicante.
- *Bullfighting is still a popular spectator sport.*
- *Waving a red rag at a bull is supposed to make it angry. But bulls are colour blind, so the matador's cape can be any colour!*

The tourist resort of Benidorm on the Costa Blanca.
- *Beaches become very crowded in summer.*
- *Tall hotel blocks are as close to the beach as possible.*

The world's largest *frontón* is in Miami, USA, with over 5000 seats for the audience.

Bullfighting is a sport that dates from the Middle Ages. It began as a sport for noblemen on horseback. Now bulls are specially bred to be killed in the arena. This is done by a *matador* and his or her assistants, the *picadores* and *banderilleros.*

At first, the bull is weakened and made angry by spikes that are stuck in its neck. Then, when the *matador* has tired it out, using a red cape to make it charge, the bull is killed with a sword. This spectator sport is enjoyed by large audiences though many people think it is cruel and should be stopped.

Just relaxing

Spanish people enjoy relaxing by taking a walk in the early evening after work, as the day becomes cooler. Some sit outside cafés, play cards or just watch everyone else. Reading is a popular way to relax.

Going to the beach is as popular with Spanish people as with visitors from other countries. Also, Spaniards regularly visit the countryside to stay with relatives in villages and on farms. They call this 'going to the village'. Skiing (in the Pyrenees, the Sierras outside Madrid, or the Sierra Nevada near Granada), is a more recent and increasingly popular holiday.

CUSTOMS AND ARTS

The annual horse fair at Jerez.
- *People enjoy dressing up and showing off their traditional costumes.*
- *Spain has a tradition of brilliant horse trainers and riders.*

Flamenco

Flamenco is the best known Spanish music. It came from the folk music of the **Gypsies** in Andalucía. It has spread to most parts of Spain as a popular form of entertainment. *Flamenco* songs are usually performed by solo singers or guitarists, or by the two together. *Flamenco* dancers join in the music by clapping their hands, clicking their fingers and stamping their feet as they dance. *Flamenco* songs often begin slowly and build up to an exciting finish.

Festivals and feasts

Festivals and feasts, called *fiestas,* are celebrated as part of the Roman Catholic religion. There are about 3000 *fiestas* in Spain each year. Most Spanish people are Roman Catholic and take their faith very seriously. Easter and Corpus Christi are two of the main events in the religious year. At each event there are street processions with decorated floats and flowers are laid out in patterns on the streets.

In Seville, there is a fair every April. People dress in their best traditional costume and ride horses through streets lined with coloured lanterns.

Saints' days called *santos* are celebrated instead of birthdays. Those who have the same name as that saint are given gifts. Also, villages or towns have their own patron saint, and have a feast day on the saint's day. In the town of Santiago de Compostela, 25 July is the feast day of St James. For hundreds of years pilgrims have travelled to the tomb of St James from all over Europe. Now the week-long feast is popular with both modern-day pilgrims and tourists.

Artists and writers

Spain has produced many famous artists, such as Salvador Dalí and Joan Miró. Some artists have based their work on events in the history of Spain. The painters Goya and Picasso painted scenes from wars they saw in Spain. Picasso lived through the Spanish **Civil War** in the 1930s. One of the world's best collections of paintings is in the Prado Art Museum in Madrid.

One of the world's first novels is by the 17th century Spanish writer, Cervantes. It is about the fantasies and adventures of a knight named Don Quixote [kee-HOtay]. In this century, the famous Spanish poet and playwright, García Lorca, was shot and killed by the **Fascists** during the Civil War.

People dress up as Moors or Christians to walk through the streets of Seville.

- *The festival is a reminder of when Christians fought the Moors for control of Spain.*

The Gypsy people first came to Spain from India in the 15th century. The Gypsy community is a close-knit one and Gypsies usually marry other Gypsies. This has helped to keep going the Gypsy traditions such as *flamenco*.

SPAIN FACTFILE

Area 504, 782 square km

Highest point on mainland
Mt Mulhacen (in the Sierra Nevada)
3478 m

Climate

	January temp.	July temp.	Total annual rainfall
Madrid	5°C	25°C	419 mm
Bilbao	9°C	19°C	1208 mm
Seville	13°C	26°C	559 mm

Population 36.7 million

Population density 78 people per square km

Life expectancy
Female 80 years
Male 74 years

Capital city Madrid

Total Population living in towns and cities 76%

Population of the main cities (in millions)

Madrid	3.0
Barcelona	1.6
Valencia	0.8
Seville	0.7
Zaragoza	0.6
Malaga	0.5
Bilbao	0.4
Las Palmas	0.3
Murcia	0.3
Palma de Mallorca	0.3

Land use

Farming	51%
Forest	32%
Other	17%

Employment

Services	56%
Industry	33%
Farming	11%

Main imports
Machinery and transport equipment
Manufactured goods
Chemicals
Food

Main exports
Machinery and transport equipment
Manufactured goods
Food
Chemicals
Fuels

Language

Spanish	70%
Catalan	21%
Galician	7%
Basque	1%
Other	1%

Religions

Roman Catholic	94%
Muslim	1%
Other and non-religious	5%

Money
The Spanish peseta

Wealth $13,650
(The total value of what is produced by the country in one year, divided by its population and converted into US dollars).

GLOSSARY

capital city the city where a country has its government

citrus fruits fruits such as oranges and lemons that contain citric acid

civil war a war fought between rival groups in the same country

colonies settlements of people who have left their home country for another country

communications how people travel or come into contact with each other

conservation the protection of wildlife and vegetation or the careful use of land to protect the future of the environment

craft industries making goods by hand using traditional methods

deciduous trees trees that shed their leaves at the end of their growing season

dictator a single ruler with complete power over a country

drought a long period without rain

fascist a member of a political group wanting to make people obey their authority

fermentation using yeast to convert the sugar in grapes to alcohol

ferry boats boats that link two places that are not too far apart, with regular sailings

food processing changing a crop or animal into food

garrigue scrub and grass in a very dry area

Gypsy member of a wandering people who originally came from India

holiday resorts towns which people go to for a holiday

import taxes money charged to a supplier for bringing goods into a country to sell

irrigation watering system set up to water the land

lava molten rock that flows out of a volcano

mass produced describes one of many identical items made in large quantites, usually in a factory

matorral trees scrub and grass in a dry area

monarchy a country that has a king or queen

national park a large area of natural landscape that is conserved for wildlife and that tourists can visit

package holiday a type of holiday which is bought by tourists and includes accommodation and return flights, in one 'package' price

peasants people who live off small amounts of land

peninsula a long area of land that is surrounded on three sides by the sea

plateau a flat-topped upland area surrounded by steep slopes

republic a country without a monarch

sierras mountain ranges

standard of living the measure of how well people live and eat in a country

temperate a climate that has no extremes of heat or cold

toll the tax charged to those who use the motorway

INDEX

Alhambra Palace 10
Alicante 11, 26
Andalucía 4, 9
artists and writers 29

Balearic Islands 6, 8, 11, 21, 25
Barcelona 5, 11, 18, 22, 24, 26, 30
Basque region 5, 26
Benidorm 11, 27
Bilbao 22, 30
bull farms and bullfighting 16, 17, 26, 27

Cabrera 6
Canary Islands 7, 11, 25
Cantabrian Mountains 6
car industry 23
Catalonia 5, 11
Cervantes 29
civil war 5, 29
climate 8, 14, 30
Costa del Azahar 12
Costa Blanca 11, 19
Costa del Sol 8, 11
Coto Doñana National Park 9
craft industries 22
culture and the arts 28, 29

daily life 12–13, 16–17
Dalí, Salvador 29
Duero river 7

European Union (EU) 5, 23

farming 7, 9, 14-15, 16, 17
festivals 4, 28–9
fishing 15
flamenco 28, 29
food and cooking 13, 18, 19, 20–1
Formentera 6
Franco, General 5

Great Mosque 10
Gross National Product (GNP) 19
Guadiana river 7
Gypsies 28, 29

history 4–5

Iberian peninsula 4
Ibiza 6
imports and exports 30
industries 22–3
irrigation 7, 15

Jerez de la Frontera 14, 28

languages 5, 30
leisure and entertainment 26–7
living standards 18
Lorca, García 29

Madrid 9, 10, 18, 22, 24, 25, 27, 29, 30
Mahón 21
Majorca 6, 25
Malaga 11, 30
Menorca 6, 21
Meseta 6, 7, 8, 15
Miró, Joan 29

Moors 4, 10, 11, 15, 29

Palma de Mallorca 25, 30
Pamplona 16
pelota 26
Picasso, Pablo 29
Pico del Teide 7
population 4, 30
Prado Art Museum 29
Pyrenees Mountains 6, 25, 27

railway network 24, 25
Real Madrid 26
religion 28, 30
rivers 7
roads and motorways 24

Santander 25
Santiago de Compostela 4, 29
Segovia 10
Seville 4, 5, 24, 25, 28, 29, 30
shops 18–19
Sierra Nevada 6, 27
siesta 19, 21
sport 26, 27

Tagus river 7
Tenerife 7, 25
tourism 8, 11, 25, 27
transport 24–5

Valencia 12, 13, 20, 30
vegetation 9

wildlife 9
wine 14, 22